Uff Da!

Let's Dance!

Scandinavian Fiddle Tunes & House Party Music

for Mandolin

MB20971

by Dix Bruce

"Uff da" is a mild exclamation used by Norwegian Americans in a variety of surprising, embarassing, or difficult situations. "Uff da" is like "Oh my gosh"! or "oh dear!" You say "uff da" when you back into the boss' car or when your wife whispers at a dinner party, "Ole, you got some lettuce stuck to your front teeth, uff da." You might say "uff da" under your breath as you realize that the "old friend" you are chatting with at the grocery store is not whom you thought he was. You have no idea who this person is and he hasn't a clue who you are, uff da. In this context of this book, "uff da" means something like "Oh well, life is life, let's dance!"

— Bruce Bollerud

Recording produced by Dix Bruce. Music engraving and book by Dix Bruce.
Special thanks to Brian Lambert and Sherry Shachter for their suggestions.

FREE

Free audio available online!
Visit: www.melbay.com/20971

BILL'S MUSIC SHELF

Contents

CD Contents

Introduction

I grew up in the Midwest, specifically in northern Michigan and southern Wisconsin. In the 1950s and 60s, at least in my part of the world, the two main ethnic groups were Norwegian and German. I inherited some genes from both, my father's parents were Norwegian, my mother's German and English. Within those relatively narrow confines, I was exposed to a range of culture.

By the time I was a teenager, my family had moved to Madison, Wisconsin. Though there was ample opportunity to explore my ethnic roots further, I had little interest in things that seemed so familiar. The great outer world of television and rock and roll loomed large and made the local scene seem boring. Even then, manure spreader ads on the TV constantly reminded me that I was not a surfer dude or a cool kid from New York City.

My attitude began to change in my college years during the early 1970s when I heard a musical trio called the Goose Island Ramblers. Their music was a mixture of many styles from western and bluegrass to Hawaiian and Norwegian, from Swiss to polka, county to swing, and everything in between or on either side. The Geese's music was pure joy delivered with passion and humor and not a trace of self consciousness.

I began hanging out at Johnny's Packer Inn, where the Geese had a weekly gig. Eventually I got to know them and their music and interviewed them for a school project. Their eclectic repertoire and straight forward style of performing entertained me immensely and truly changed my life. They introduced me to untold numbers of great songs and styles of music. They reintroduced me to my Midwestern roots and made them interesting, fun, and exciting. I'll forever be in their debt as I continue to record their songs and include them in my instructional books.

I eventually settled in California but always kept in touch with Bruce Bollerud the accordion player, George Gilbertsen the fiddler, mandolinist, dobro player, and Wendy Whitford, guitarist and fiddler. They all sang and wrote songs. On a visit back to Wisconsin in the late 1990s, I mentioned to Bruce Bollerud that if he ever wanted to put any of the Geese's music down on paper, I'd be interested in helping with the project.

Bruce thought about it and decided that he wanted to set down some of the traditional music he'd played all of his life, music he felt was in danger of fading away as the old timers who inherited it from the previous generation passed on. Bruce called it "Norwegian House Party Music."

Mostly fiddle-based, house party music was played out in the country in an era when farmers would go to their neighbor's houses for weekend entertainment. It was usually played by a small string combo with a fiddle, maybe some kind of accordion and a guitar or banjo. You can read more about house party music and the individual tunes in this book in my interview with Bruce on page 7.

By the late 1940s, country folk began coming to town on the weekends to shop, see movies, or dance to the hot new regional polka bands. The polka bands were "the latest thing," larger and louder, horn-based, and there was really no place in them for the old time sound of the fiddle. The country culture changed and as a result, house party music began to fade away. Of course, the old timers continued to play their tunes but there weren't many younger string players interested in learning the old time music.

Bruce Bollerud, who plays a variety of instruments including accordion and bandonion, learned the house party repertoire as a young teen backing up local fiddlers. As he moved on to other bands and styles, he always mixed in a little of the old time music with the newer repertoire. When he met Wendy and George and joined the Goose Island Ramblers in the 1960s, he found kindred spirits with whom to swap tunes. Each knew a thousand old tunes that they taught each other and began to perform. Bruce wanted to collect some of these in the hope that new generations of players would discover them and have as much fun as he has had playing them.

I had never heard most of these tunes until I recorded Bruce playing them for his Mel Bay book "Uff Da! Let's Dance! *Scandinavian House Party Tunes for Accordion.*" I grew to love them as I mixed and edited the recording. I told Bruce I wanted to learn some of them. He said he hoped I'd take the tunes and put together a mandolin book. Sounded like a good idea and a great way to get more acquainted with the repertoire. You hold the result in your hands!

As I mentioned, I would never have heard these tunes if it weren't for Bruce and the Goose Island Ramblers. Again I thank them. I specifically want to thank Bruce for his generosity in sharing this wonderful music with me and now with all of you. So, it's time to tuck into the music. You'll have a ball, or maybe a house party!

Visit me online at www.musixnow.com. My e-mail address is: dix@musixnow.com.

Dix Bruce
July 2005

Dix Bruce is a musician and writer from the San Francisco Bay Area. He has authored nearly fifty books, recordings, and videos for Mel Bay Publications. He edited Mandolin World News, David Grisman's legendary mandolin magazine, from 1978 to 1984. Dix performs and does studio work on guitar, mandolin, and banjo and has recorded two LPs with mandolin legend Frank Wakefield, eight big band CDs with the Royal Society Jazz Orchestra, his own collection of American folk songs entitled "My Folk Heart" on which he plays guitar, mandolin, autoharp and sings, and a CD of string swing and jazz entitled "Tuxedo Blues." He has released four CDs of traditional American songs and originals with guitarist Jim Nunally, most recently a collection of "brother duet" style recordings entitled "Brothers at Heart." His most recent mandolin works include "The Parking Lot Picker's Songbook for Mandolin", "Gypsy Swing & Hot Club Rhythm for Mandolin I and II", "Getting into Bluegrass Mandolin" and "First Lessons: Mandolin DVD." Dix has just released a DVD entitled "Swing & Jazz Mandolin: Chords & Songs." For project updates, log on to www.musixnow.com or contact Musix, PO Box 231005, Pleasant Hill, CA 94523.

Also by Dix Bruce

For songlists and full details, as well as info on new books, CDs and DVDs, log on to www.musixnow.com

Music instruction:

Getting into Bluegrass Mandolin book and CD

First Lessons: Mandolin book, CD, & DVD

You Can Teach Yourself Mandolin book & CD, DVD or video set.

Parking Lot Picker's Songbooks for Mandolin, Guitar, & Banjo (with Bill Evans)

You Can Teach Yourself Country Guitar book & CD, DVD or video set.

BackUp Trax: Old Time Fiddle Tunes Vol. I book & CD set. Jam all night long with the band on old time and fiddle tunes.

Basic Swing Guitar (video)

Basic Country Flatpicking Guitar (video) Explores easy Carter-style solos.

BackUp Trax: Swing & Jazz Vol. I book & CD set. Jam all night long with a great band. You play all the leads and the band never gets tired!

BackUp Trax: Traditional Jazz & Dixieland book & CD set. Jam all night long with the band on the basic Dixieland repertoire.

BackUp Trax: Early Jazz & Hot Tunes book & CD set. Jam all night long with the band on more traditional jazz standards.

Recordings:

Brothers at Heart CD by Dix Bruce & Jim Nunally of brother duet-style song, & hot guitar picking (FGM CD 111)

From Fathers to Sons CD by Dix Bruce & Jim Nunally of folk, bluegrass, & hot guitar picking (Musix CD/C 104).

The Way Things Are CD by Dix Bruce & Jim Nunally. More hot picking & great new songs by the duo. (Musix CD 105).

My Folk Heart CD by Dix Bruce, solo & small group, traditional American folk music (Musix CD/C101). With Jim Nunally, Tom Rozum, and John Reischman.

Tuxedo Blues CD by Dix Bruce, string swing & jazz (Musix CD/C102). With Bob Alekno on mandolin, David Balakrishnan on violin, Mike Wollenberg on bass.

The Tunes and Where They Come From

I interviewed Bruce Bollerud in April 2002. I asked him about the House Party era and also about each of the tunes in this book. My questions and his answers are below. My comments on playing the individual tunes on mandolin follow in parenthesis and italics.

– Dix Bruce

Photo: Dix Bruce

Bruce Bollerud 2002

Dix Bruce: Tell us about house party music.

Bruce Bollerud: I lived on a farm in south western Wisconsin, and heard house party music at our house and at neighbors' houses. There were dances on weekend nights in people's homes, rural people playing music. You'd go to the neighbor's farm, they'd roll back the rug in the parlor — they didn't have wall to wall carpeting in those days, they just had a rug — sometimes they'd move the kitchen stove right out into the yard. They'd make as much room as they could for dancing. And then, the little band, which would be a two or three piece outfit usually, would set up in a corner and play.

DB: What was the instrumentation of these bands?

BB: They'd always have a guitar for the rhythm, sometimes it could be a banjo, plus a fiddle and an accordion. It'd be some combination of those instruments. Sometimes it might be a guitar and a fiddle, sometimes it might be a guitar and an accordion.

DB: The guitar player probably didn't take leads.

BB: No. He was strictly rhythm. The lead players would play in unison. I don't think they played harmonies that much. Some did, but not that much. Three, four minutes per song, probably, as long as people danced.

DB: How did they mix up the different kinds of tunes?

BB: More waltzes than anything, old time waltzes. And then they would throw in a schottische or two, more waltzes, and then maybe a polka, more waltzes and a two-step. The waltzes were fiddle waltzes with a certain sound from the bow work. Three chord songs, most of them, they weren't too complicated. They were rhythmic, they had a certain tempo and a certain swing that the Norwegian waltzes have. They could be Norwegian, Swedish, I don't think so much Danish. There weren't many Danes in the area where I grew up.

DB: Did this music come from a fiddle tradition in the old country?

BB: Absolutely. The fiddle is kind of the national instrument of Scandinavia. The accordion came along a little later in the 1830s, I suppose.

DB: In your introduction to your accordion book "Uff Da! Let's Dance! *Scandinavian House Party Tunes for Accordion"* you said that you came along kind of at the tail end of the house party era.

BB: This would be in the middle to late forties and maybe the early fifties. It was a gradual process, but as the automobile came in and became more common, people began to go farther for a night's entertainment. Before that, they had stayed right in their own little neighborhoods and their own little towns. Once the car came in, they began to travel to the next town, and somebody realized they could put on a dance at a hall and maybe get two, three hundred people to come in, charge them a buck a piece, pay the band, and make some money. So, when that began to happen it was sort of the "in" thing. House parties were local to each little rural community but people began to go to the hall dances further away.

DB: Did people pay to go to the house parties?

BB: They usually passed the hat for the band. People brought food and drink. There'd be a lunch served. They were invitational parties, farmers would invite the neighbors and friends and some relatives. You might have twenty or thirty people, maybe, at a big house party. And you knew everybody there. If a stranger walked in, he'd better know somebody. There wasn't going to be any harm come to him, but he'd get the cold shoulder. House parties were fairly temperate, I would say, except that somebody would sometimes have a jug out in the milk house, or behind a tree. It might be home brew: home made wine or whatever. Some of the guys would sneak out and have a sip or two. They were pretty careful not to get too liquored up.

DB: Was it during WWII that you were first exposed to house party music?

BB: Yes. The house parties might have had a slight resurgence around that time because a lot of the musicians were gone to the service.

DB: Why did the fiddle tradition fade out?

BB: When the hall dances started up, when the Six Fat Dutchmen and Frankie Yankovic and all these guys became popular, the cool thing was to go to those dances. I can remember when I was a young guy, in my teens, still in high school, I'd go to the dances. That's where the girls were, for one thing, and the music was exciting. You had a ten-piece brass band up there putting out a lot of stuff, and they were good. I think the fiddle music couldn't compete with it on that level at that time, volume-wise, and it wasn't considered cool. For a time during the transition to accordion and brass band, there were bands that had a fiddle. They would have drums and trumpet or sax, some combination of horns. But these eventually faded out.

DB: Are the keys that you play these tunes in the original fiddle keys?

BB: Mostly. Fiddlers like sharp keys (G, A, D) etc. Part of that is the sound they get with those open strings on the fiddle and they ring more.

DB: When you play these songs you seem the have a specific idea of what tempo to play each tune at.

How did you develop that? Where does it come from?

BB: I don't know, you just kind of feel it. It's like if somebody would ask you, "How do you know when to change chord from D to G?" or whatever it might be. How do you actually know that? I couldn't tell you how I actually "know" that. I know it's going to happen, I know I have to go to G next. I can't give you a rule for the tempos.

DB: It must go back to playing for dancers.

BB: Within certain parameters. There's a certain feeling. Like with a Viennese waltz, kind of a majestic feeling almost. The Norwegian waltzes have kind of an earthiness to them.

DB: Before you mentioned the term "swing."

BB: The Norwegian waltzes swing. Of course all music swings if it's good.

DB: How did you learn these songs? By repetition with the fiddlers you played with?

BB: Mostly, yes. I think music is made up of a lot of cliches and a particular style will have particular little cliches that tend to happen again and again. You can kind of string them together, or at least that's the way I've organized it. The first thing I usually do if I'm learning a piece is to get the chord progression down so I know where it's going to change. And then I start picking out the melody.

DB: Talk about the individual tunes.

BB: Kjarring Og Mann Slust or "The Old Man and his Wife Fighting." That's a song I learned from Everett Kittleson and he learned it from Orville Rundhaug and I don't know where Orville got it from. It's a two part song, and the way Everett explained it to me is that the first part is calm and easy going. That's the man. The second part is a little more chattery and that's the woman. It's kind of a little joke! At least the men laugh when they hear that explanation. *(DB: Tremolo allows a mandolinist to extend any note indefinitely, just like the violinist's bow. I added tremolo on longer notes on several of the tunes. In "Kjarring Og Mann Slust" I played tremolo on dotted halves and tied dotted halves. Feel free to experiment with tremolo on your own. My inclusions are only suggestions. The numbers between the standard notation and the tablature denote fretting finger numbers: 1 = index, 2= middle, 3 = ring, 4 = fourth.)*

The Goose Island Ramblers ca. 1964,
l to r: George Gilbertsen, Wendy Whitford, Bruce Bollerud

As Bruce mentions, all of these tunes are best performed with a sort of "swing." It's not exactly "swing" in the Benny Goodman or Count Basie sense, but it's related as far as danceability. It's relaxed and loose and often evolves as the performance progresses. The easiest way to explain it is to look at a pair of consecutive eighth notes. They're not played with equal emphasis or strict time value. Rather, the first of the notes will be given a bit more lilt and accent and held a bit longer than the second.

*So, instead of a "dut-dut-dut-dut" feel, go for more of a "**DUT**-dut-**DUT**-dut." "Swing" eighth note pairs are often written as a dotted eighth followed by a sixteenth. We decided not to use that convention both because it can be difficult to read and because it tends too imply a stricter rhythmic feel. And, some tunes swing more than others, some swing very little if at all. As you listen to the CD, pay particular attention to the feel and swing of each tune.* (Page 16)

Sally's Hoppwaltz Polka. "Sally" is actually Selmer Oren but they called him Sally as a nickname, and he was an old time fiddler. He had a lot of good pieces and that was one that he played. I didn't learn it from him though, I learned it from Art Leuten from Stoughton, Wisconsin, who had learned it from him, and it's just a real good hoppwaltz. A hoppwaltz is not a waltz, it's a polka. They dance to it with like a Polish hop, and the Norwegians have always called that a "hoppwaltz." Whoever named it must have seen some similarity with the steps of the waltz. The hoppwaltz has a step pattern that goes, "1—2—3" then a hop. That could explain the term "hoppwaltz " since the waltz also goes "1—2—3." And, "Sally's Hoppwaltz Polka" is not in 3/4 time, it's a polka in 2/4. (Page 18)

The Stegen Waltz means "The Step Ladder Waltz." The first part is basically the same tune as "Tobacco Setter's Waltz," with just a little alteration. Don't you think that's kind of odd to name a waltz after a step ladder? *(DB: Fiddlers and mandolinists often use "double stops" in their playing. On the mandolin we play a double stop when we fret and pick two notes at the same time. "Stegen Waltz" has double stops in measures 8, 9, 17, and 18. [Measure numbers are shown above the treble clef sign on each staff except the first.] Fretting finger numbers for double stops are stacked. The number on top shows which finger to use to fret the higher note, the number on the bottom shows which finger to use to fret the lower note.)* (Page 19)

Red Rooster Two Step. (The late) Wendy Whitford played that for George (Gilbertsen) and I when we recorded in 1999 and we said, "When did you learn that Wendy?" He said, "Aw, I played that fifty years ago," or whatever it was. We said, "Well, you never played it for us." He said, "I guess I didn't." We said, "How come?" He said, "Well I guess I didn't think of it!" Here was a song that he'd had for years. We'd played together for thirty five years (as the Goose Island Ramblers) and never heard that song. No telling how many other songs he might have had. "Red Rooster" is a ragtime piece and it's interesting that the second part is in a minor key. It's neat that string band musicians listened to ragtime music, which was popular in the day. I wonder how the title came about. (Page 20)

DB: You learned a lot of these songs from Wendy Whitford. Could you talk a little bit about how Wendy learned them and how he passed them on to you?

BB: I'm sure that he played along with some of these old fiddlers that were old when he was young (in the 1920s and 1930s). He mentions Ryerson, Ole Gutrud, and George Matson, a whole bunch of people that I never knew but heard about forever. They were probably playing at a house party and he probably sat down beside them, watched their fingers and listened. He did a remarkable job. He wasn't a Norwegian, but when he played those Norwegian pieces, he was Norwegian in his heart. He really felt that music.

Skjorte Frak Waltz is the "Shirt Tail Waltz." I don't know the significance of that. I kind of see in my mind's eye somebody dancing all night long and maybe a guy's shirt came out, or something like that, kind of flopping around as he was dancing. *(DB: In this style of music, modulations are quite common. They add a great deal of harmonic interest. "Skjorte Frak Waltz" begins in the key of G and modulates* *to the key of D.)* (Page 22)

Herman's Schottische in D I learned from Herman Erickson, who was the first fiddle player that I played with. I didn't know it at the time, but later on I heard George Gilbertsen play a similar tune "Flop Eared Mule," which he calls "The Big Eared Mule." A lot of people play "Flop Eared Mule" as a hoe-down tune. Herman played it as a schottische, and I've heard some other Norwegians play it that way. I suspect they heard this hoe-down tune, slowed it down, and turned it into a schottische. And it works very well. *(DB: Just like "Flop Eared Mule," "Herman's Schottische in D" modulates from the key of D to the key of A.)* (Page 24)

DB: There are several songs here that mention Ryerson. Who was Ryerson?

BB: He was an old fiddler, I think it was Clarence Ryerson, who Wendy Whitford used to listen to when Wendy was young. He must have been a crackerjack because all of his pieces are good.

DB: Was **Ryerson's Hoppwaltz** the name that Ryerson had for the song?

BB: I doubt it very much. These guys didn't name pieces after themselves very often. He probably called it something else, might have been "Olson's Waltz" or whatever. Wendy knew it as "Ryerson's." *(DB: If you have difficulty playing the double stops in measures 8, 9, 17, and 18, leave out the bottom note and just play the D melody note.)* (Page 25)

Gra Lysining means "the gray light of morning." I learned that from Herman Erickson too. These house parties would last all night long, and people would be walking or driving home in the *gra lysining*. Getting light, but the sun isn't up yet. *(DB: I played tremolo on half notes or longer. You might try adding a second note to these to make a double stop. The rule of thumb is to add a chord tone above or below the melody note. In measure sixteen try adding the open second string A to the fretted A melody note. In measures twenty and twenty eight, add the first string, second fret F# to the D. In measures twenty two and thirty, add the second string, second fret B to the E.)* (Page 26)

Auction Pa Strommen. "Strommen" is a Norwegian name, and Wendy told me that they went down to Strommen's place for an auction and it rained that day. So, the auction kind of fizzled out and they went in the house and had a house party. They played the fiddle. I'm not sure who was playing the fiddle, if it was Ryerson or one of those old guys that Wendy talked about, but that was one of the pieces and Wendy learned it. It's an unusual piece because the first part is in C and the second part goes to D. Usually you'd go from C to G or C to F, but C, right into D is unusual. It's kind of neat though because the second half of the second part goes up to G temporarily and then back down to D. And then, when you go back to C, you just drop down from D to C. Unusual for an old time tune. *(DB: I used tremolo for dotted half notes in the slow version of "Auction Pa Strommen" but not in the regular speed recording. Listen to both and see which you like better.)* (Page 28)

Johnny Homme's Waltz. Johnny Homme was a neighbor of ours from Hollandale, lived about a mile and a half away. He was an old fiddler and we played a few house parties together and that was one that he played. I'm real sorry that I didn't record more of his stuff. Most of the old fiddler's were a little rough, their technique wasn't real tight, but he was very smooth and accurate in what he did. I'm sure I lost a lot of good pieces there that I didn't get, and he's dead now, so they're gone. (Page 30)

Minnesota 6/8 Two Step. I met this fiddle band, two fiddles, a banjo, and a guitar, from Mabel, Minnesota. Erik Bye, a big television producer and star in Norway, had come over here to America to tape programs of Norwegian American musicians, artists, and craftspeople for Norwegian television. He called me and asked me to come up to Minneapolis and play on this show. I thought that was kind of neat because they got to see me in Norway. While I was up there, I met these old fellows who were playing these tunes and they gave me a tape of their stuff. "Minnesota 6/8 Two Step" was learned from them. (Page 32)

Sentimental Selma. There was a big Scandinavian dialect humor thing going on from the teens (1911-1919), and up, and they did songs either in Norwegian or Swedish, and they also did them in English with a comic Scandinavian accent, and this was one of those. My mother's name was Selma, so I think of her whenever I play it. In the song, Sentimental Selma "went to Hollywood to act like Greta Garbo," who was a Swede, of course. "Barnum said she could." Then it goes, "I think you are the cutest girl I ever knew, your sunny smile thrills me through and through. Yeah, well, Selma you don't have to tell me, your eyes and your smile, *yust* like yesterday." I imagine in my mind that she went out there to Hollywood to try to make it big and maybe she didn't quite make it, maybe she came back sometime later, and maybe this guy is still carrying the torch for her. English lyrics set to a traditional tune.
It was a schottische. The melody had been around a long time. And there are Norwegian lyrics. I've heard several different sets of lyrics in Norwegian. (In Norwegian) *Huk si du en dagen/Jeg møte deg på isen/Da du drogge/den gra stygge griesen.* That means, "Do you remember the day I met you on the ice? When you were dragging the old gray pig." (Page 33)

Art's Waltz is from Art Lewton of Stoughton, Wisconsin. I think he got it from a man by the name of Andrew Kleven. That's as much as he knew about it. These tunes are really handed from one musician to the next. I'm sure somebody "wrote" them at some point back, but it might be a long time ago. You might be looking at a hundred years ago. (Page 34)

Almando's Polka. Almando was one of the guys from the Mabel, Minnesota, fiddle band, I can't remember his last name, but I had talked mostly with him and he gave me most of these things. *(DB: "Almando's Polka" has a nice modulation from the key of G to the key of D. This isn't one of the easiest tunes to play due to many position and fingering shifts.)* (Page 36)

Abner Juve's Waltz. Abner Juve was another man I didn't know, but somebody that Wendy had heard when he was young. Wendy played a few of his songs. *(DB: Tremolo works nicely on the longer notes. Again, you can add a second note, a simple chord tone, at these points to create a double stop. In measures four, twelve, twenty one and twenty nine, add the open second string A to the melody E. In measures eight and twenty four, add the open second string A to the melody F#. In measure sixteen, add the open second string A to the melody D. In measures twenty and twenty eight, add the second string, second fret B to the melody G. Fret the B with your first finger, the G with your third. In measures twenty two and thirty, add the open first string E to the C# melody note.)* (Page 38)

Mabel's Rag Two Step and **Mabel Polka** are two more tunes from the Mabel, Minnesota, fiddle band. (Page 40)

Ryerson's Waltz. Another tune learned from Wendy Whitford, who learned it from Clarence Ryerson. (Page 42)

Art's Schottische. Another tune learned from Art Lewton of Stoughton, Wisconsin. (Page 44)

Grandpa's Waltz. I'm not sure, but the "grandpa" referred to in the titles could be Wendy Whitford's grandfather. Same with **Grandpa's Mazurka**. (Page 45) I kind of doubt that Wendy's grandpa would have written either. He probably just liked those tunes and Wendy named them according to that. *(DB: Try tremolo on the longer notes.)* (Page 46)

Old Utica Waltz is one that Wendy Whitford played and he learned it from one of those old fiddlers, I don't know who. He thought the name of it was the "Old Utica Waltz." It may or may not be the "Old Utica Waltz," but that's what he called it. (Page 50)

Johnny's Swiss Polka is from Johnny Mueller. He played the bandonion. He had given me the music to it except that it wasn't written out in notes. He used a number system that had a series of dots to indicate how long a note should be held. *(DB: Three different keys in "Johnny's Swiss Polka"! The fourth part, starting in measure twenty seven, reminds me of the tune "Little Brown Jug.")* (Page 52)

Johnson's Rhinelander Schottische. There's no specific "Johnson," it's kind of a generic title. I had that song on tape and Gilbert Prestebroten announced the name of it but I can't make it out because somebody coughed or something just as he said it. It was something like "Johnson," not really Johnson, but I just tacked it on. You gotta have *something* on there! The "Rhinelander" is a style of schottische. The influence came from Germany, I'm sure. *(DB: Note the modulation from the key of F to the key of C.)* (Page 54)

Cousin Olin's Waltz. Cousin Olin was a first cousin to my mother up in New Auburn, Wisconsin, and he played the three-row button accordion. He learned that waltz from a traveling salesman that came through selling something. Whatever it was he sold, this guy would come into town and play the accordion a little bit to get people in the mood and then present his sales pitch. It's an unusual waltz with a kind of a Hawaiian effect to it. I wonder if it was influenced by the Hawaiian music that was popular in the early part of the century. Maybe Hawaiian music drifted into the house party group too. *(DB: Try tremolo on the longer notes.)* (Page 56)

The Tobacco Setter's Waltz. When they planted the tobacco, the tobacco setters had to ride on a little rig and set the tobacco plant in the ground, each one individually. Obviously that piece had to have come from around Stoughton or Edgerton, Wisconsin, somewhere in that area where they raised tobacco. This tune is similar to "The Stegen Waltz." (Page 58)

Ole's Schottische. "Ole" is just a generic Norwegian in this particular case. There's another name on the tape that I learned the tune from, but I don't know what it is, and I had to name it something. So I named it "Ole's Schottische" for all the Oles out there. (Page 59)

Sugar Candy Schottische. *(In Norwegian: "Sukkertoy")* That I got from an accordion player from Hollandale, Wisconsin, Gilbert Prestebroten. He had some real good old time pieces and that was one of them. I had played in his band when I was sixteen years old. I had been playing with the old fiddlers, at house parties and things. Gilbert had a band before the war and during the war they kind of broke it up because most of the guys were drafted. After the war, probably in the early fifties, he decided to start a band again. He came over to our farm and I was milking a cow, and he started talking to me. And, like

Norwegians do, he talked about the weather and he talked about the crops, and he talked about this and that. Finally, he asked if I would like to play with his band. I was real excited about that, I was sixteen at the time and now I was going to go play with one of those dance hall bands. I played piano and trombone, but mostly piano with the Rhythm Ramblers. Gilbert played accordion. It was an old time dance band: polkas and waltzes and fox trots. They didn't call them "polka" bands in those days, they called them "old time" bands as opposed to "modern" bands which played "Star Dust," "In the Mood," and things like that. (Page 60)

DB: It's the classic folk process: as a new person hears and performs an old tune, the melody or harmony might be changed a little bit, and, as you've said, the titles got changed and re-arranged.

BB: Yes, they did.

DB: Most of the tunes in this set are in major keys.

BB: Most of the Norwegian or Scandinavian pieces in this country were in major keys. In the old country, they used minor keys a lot. The major key was still the predominant key but they used minors a good deal. Norwegian-American fiddle tunes are a whole different art form than the tunes played in Norway. They're related, obviously, but they're different. I think the tunes are simpler, tend to be in the major key, tend to be two part songs, as opposed to three part songs in the old country. Norwegian-American fiddlers simplified the tunes. I think they did that because they were not professional musicians. They were farmers, working people. Those old farmers had big, strong hands that probably didn't move as quick a professional musician's hands would, so they did what they could do.

DB: Why do you think the Scandinavian Americans left the minor keys largely behind?

BB: First of all, the weather. The sun doesn't shine as much over there. It's cloudier and rainier, that kind of dampens your spirits a little bit sometimes. At the time of the immigrants, back in the 1850s and before, the people were oppressed, they were poor, back in Norway. There wasn't much hope for advancement. You couldn't marry a rich man's daughter, you stayed in your own class. When they got over here, things opened up, there was hope. If you worked hard, and if you were fairly smart with how you did things, you could make some money. I think major keys are happier than minor keys. Also they may have felt they had more personal and artistic freedom in the new country. They didn't have to follow a form that was already established, they could invent their own. They didn't have to tip their hat to some minister or official of the government that came by. And, I think they heard other music. They heard American music and English music, and Irish music and German music, and they took bits and pieces from all of this and strained it through their own experience and came up with new things.

DB: What do you think the future is for these kinds of tunes?

BB: Well, it's kind of bleak, I'm afraid. The old fiddlers that play these tunes are dying off. Some of the tunes are being picked up, but not very many, and most of them haven't been written down, that I know of. There's a fairly good body of these that are recorded and they won't be lost totally in that regard. The only thing is, unless these pieces get out where the public can hear them, and unless some younger musicians take them up, they become museum pieces. That's better than nothing, because someone can always go back and pull them out, but I don't know that they will.

I think one of the things that happened here is that folk music has been popularly thought of as coming out of the South and the West, but you don't hear people talk a lot about folk music coming from the Midwest. I'm not sure why that is. Consequently, the researchers and the people like Alan Lomax and all these people who went back and recorded these obscure little tunes in the hills, didn't come up here and do that very much. So, some of that stuff has just withered on the vine.

DB: I don't know of anyone of the stature of a John or Alan Lomax or Charles Seeger looking at this culture from the outside and chronicling it the way other cultures have been recorded and collected.

BB: I don't know why they didn't look at this culture, but they didn't, apparently. It's funny. Polkas are a folk music, certainly, what else could you call them? But people who follow folk music seem to kind of look down on polkas. They don't regard it as a folk music. Maybe it's because after the house party era, polka or "old time" music was played by professional bands like Whoopie John, the Six Fat Dutchmen, and Frankie Yankovic.

DB: Do you think this Scandinavian music could find an audience outside of that ethnic community?

BB: Absolutely! I could see a bluegrass group playing this stuff like nothing! It would fit. It's in the right key and being fiddle driven, it has the right nuances.

DB: Most of this music is dance oriented. Probably what we need to do is keep people dancing and they'll continue to want this music.

BB: Of course, people don't dance the way they used to. Even bluegrass is now a concert type of music. I suspect that they may have danced to it earlier on because I don't think the tempos were quite as fast in the beginning, kind of pre-Monroe. This stuff could be jazzed up if you wanted to do it faster (for listening). I'd like to see younger musicians come in, take up this music and play it. I think of bluegrass, for example, which has been revived and carried forward by younger musicians. Musicians of national stature, like Ricky Skaggs, have come in and given it a great big boost. I don't know that that would happen here, but it would be nice. At least it would be nice if local younger musicians would play some of it before it's gone like a puff of smoke.

The Goose Island Ramblers with Dix Bruce, 9/24/1994.
l to r: Wendy Whitford, George Gilbertsen, Dix Bruce,
Bruce Bollerud.

Classic recordings by the Goose Island Ramblers are available from Cuca Records, 3838 Highway 78, Mt. Horeb, WI 93572-1116.

Kjarring Og Mann Slust

CD tracks 1 & 2

The Old Man and Woman Fighting

Arrangement © 2005 by Bruce Bollerud & Dix Bruce

20
C
24
G7
C
28
32
G7
C

Sally's Hoppwaltz

Polka

CD tracks 3 & 4

Stegen Waltz

Step Ladder Waltz

CD tracks 5 & 6

Red Rooster Two Step

CD tracks 7 & 8

22
E7
Am
27
E7
Am
E7
G7
33
C
G7
38
C
43
G7
C
(last time only)

Skjorte Frak Waltz

Shirt Tail Waltz

CD tracks 9 & 10

Arrangement © 2005 by Bruce Bollerud & Dix Bruce

17 D A7 D
21 A7 D
25 A7 D
29 A7 D

Herman's Schottische in D

CD tracks 11 & 12

Ryerson's Hoppwaltz

CD tracks 13 & 14

Gra Lysining

CD tracks 15 & 16

In the Gray Light of the Morning

17
A
D
21
E7
A
25
D
29
E7
A
A
1
2.

Auction Pa Strommen

The Auction at Strommen's

CD tracks 17 & 18

21
D
26
A7
D
33
G D A7 D G
38
D A7 D G D A7
44
D G D A7 D

Johnny Homme's Waltz

CD tracks 19 & 20

17
G
C
21
D7
G
25
C
29
D7
G

Minnesota 6/8 Two Step

CD tracks 21 & 22

Arrangement © 2005 by Bruce Bollerud & Dix Bruce

Sentimental Selma

Schottische

CD tracks 23 & 24

Art's Waltz in A

CD tracks 25 & 26

17
A
D
21
E7
A
25
D
29
E7
A

Almando's Polka

CD tracks 27 & 28

17
D
A7
21
D
25
G
29
D
A7
D

Abner Juve's Waltz

CD tracks 29 & 30

Arrangement © 2005 by Bruce Bollerud & Dix Bruce

17
D
G
21
A7
D
25
G
29
A7
D

Mabel Rag Two Step

CD tracks 31 & 32

Arrangement © 2005 by Bruce Bollerud & Dix Bruce

17
F
C7
21
F
25
C7
29
F
F
1
2.

Ryerson's Waltz

CD tracks 33 & 34

13
A7
D
17
G
D
21
A7
D
1
2.

Art's Schottische

CD tracks 35 & 36

Grandpa's Mazurka

CD tracks 37 & 38

Grandpa's Waltz

CD tracks 39 & 40

17
G
C
21
D7
G
25
C
29
D7
G

Mabel Polka

CD tracks 41 & 42

Arrangement © 2005 by Bruce Bollerud & Dix Bruce

18
F
B♭
22
C7
F
26
B♭
30
C7
F
1
2

Old Utica Waltz

CD tracks 43 & 44

18
G
D7
22
G
26
D7
30
G

Johnny's Swiss Polka

CD tracks 45 & 46

D
A7
D
A7
D
G
C
G
D7
G
C
G
D7
G
G

Johnson's Rhinelander Schottische

CD tracks 47 & 48

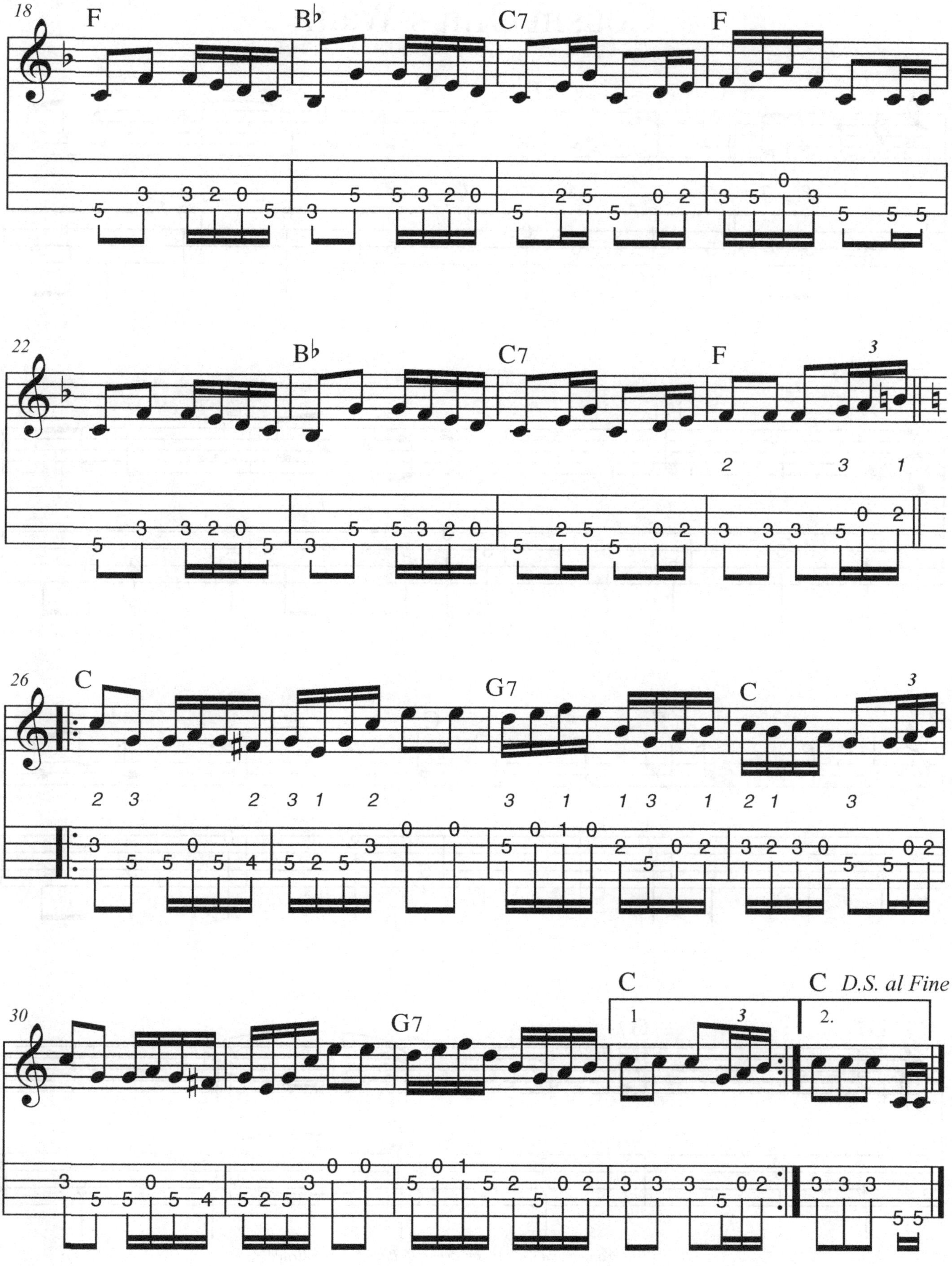
18
F
B♭
C7
F
22
B♭
C7
F
26
C
G7
C
30
G7
C
1
C
D.S. al Fine
2.

Cousin Olin's Waltz

CD tracks 49 & 50

Arrangement © 2005 by Bruce Bollerud & Dix Bruce

17
C
G7
21
C
25
G7
29
C

Tobacco Setter's Waltz

CD tracks 51 & 52

Ole's Schottische

CD tracks 53 & 54

Sugar Candy Schottische

CD tracks 55 & 56

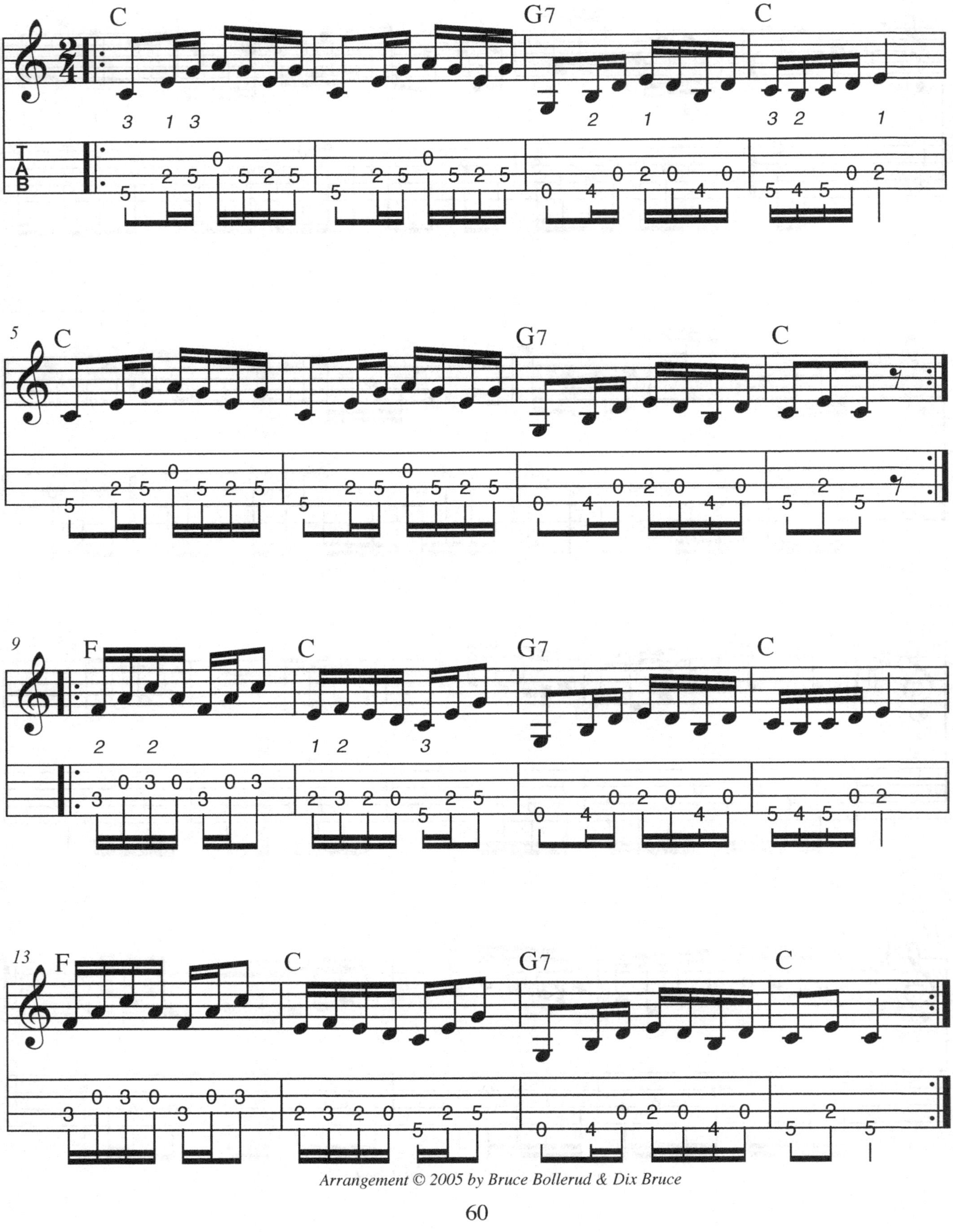

Mandolin Chord Dictionary

Reminder: All closed-position chords are moveable up and down the neck. Not all possible forms are shown for each chord, as they may be difficult to make high on the fingerboard. Be sure to try moving all forms up and down the fingerboard as far as possible on your mandolin. The "r" under a chord grid shows where the chord's "root" is located. This root note names the chord, and as you move a closed chord form, this note will identify and name the new chord. Some chord forms will not include a root note. Chords with two names separated by a slash (Cs/Df, As7/Bf7, Fsm/Gfm) are "enharmonic" names for the same chord.

Major Chords

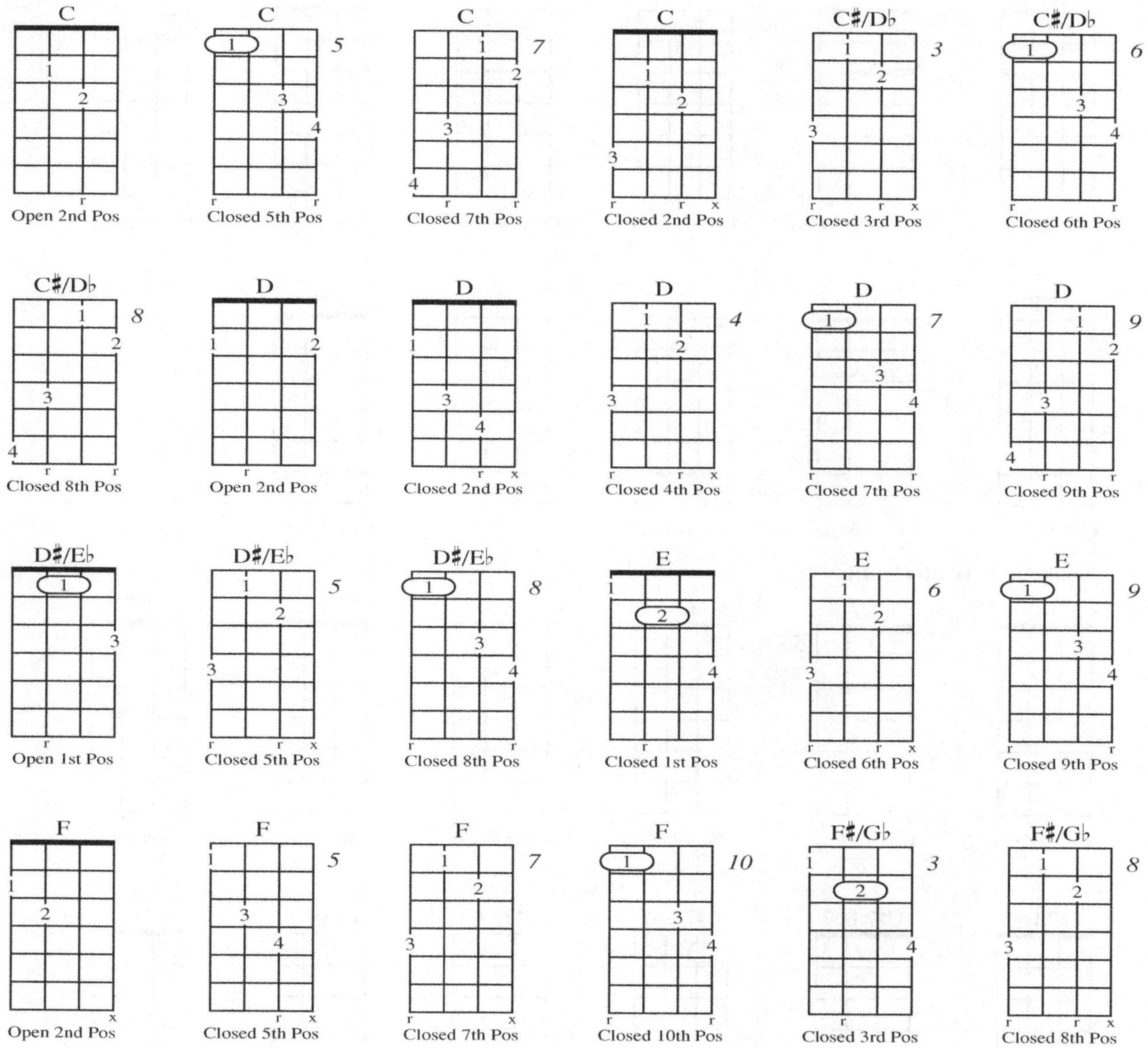

F♯/G♭

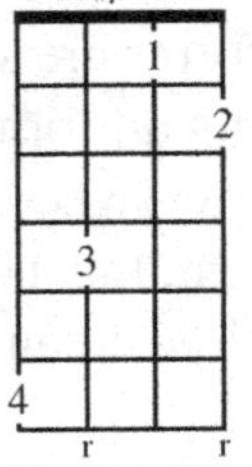

Closed 1st Pos

G

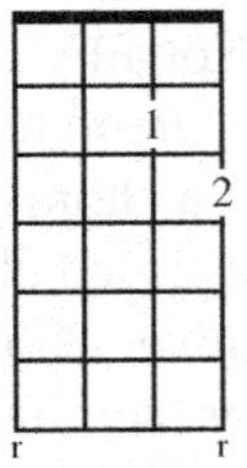

Open 2nd Pos

G

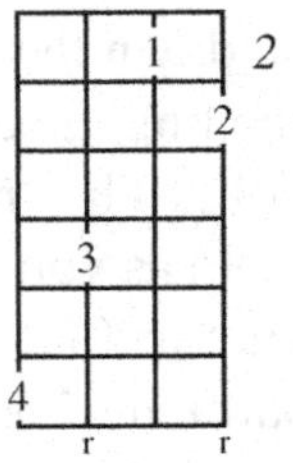

Closed 2nd Pos

G

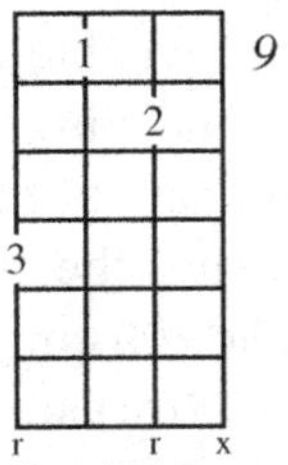

Closed 9th Pos

G♯/A♭

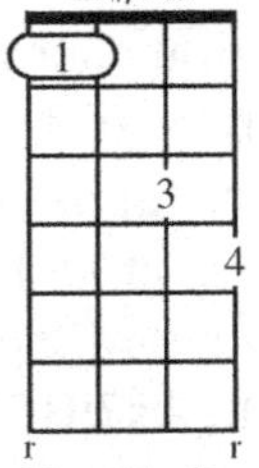

Closed 1st Pos

G♯/A♭

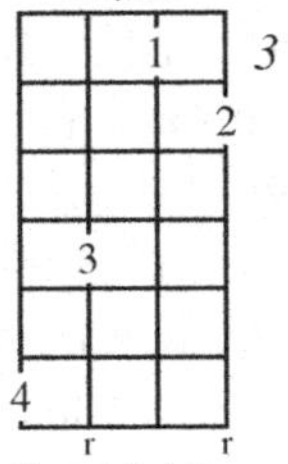

Closed 3rd Pos

G♯/A♭

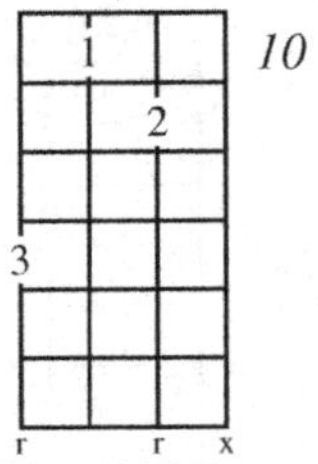

Closed 10th Pos

A

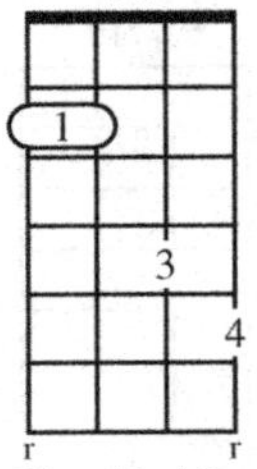

Closed 2nd Pos

A

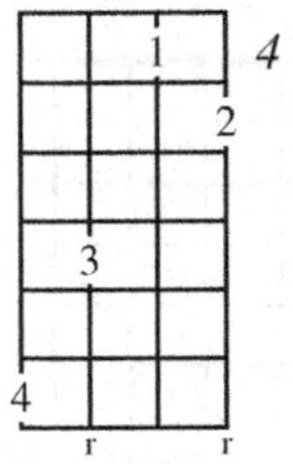

Closed 4th Pos

A

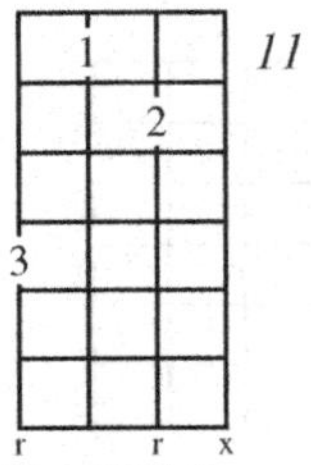

Closed 11th Pos

A♯/B♭

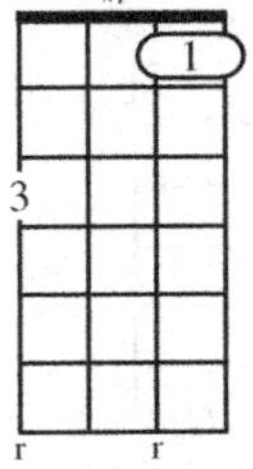

Open 1st Pos

A♯/B♭

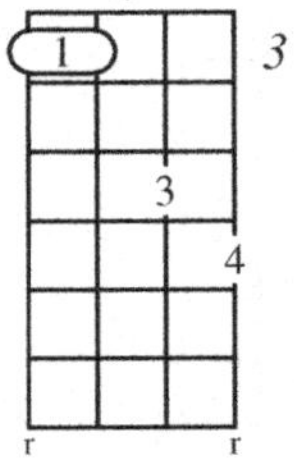

Closed 3rd Pos

A♯/B♭

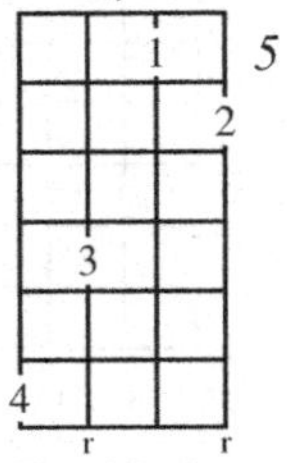

Closed 5th Pos

B

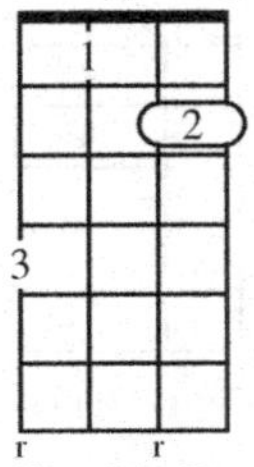

Closed 1st Pos

B

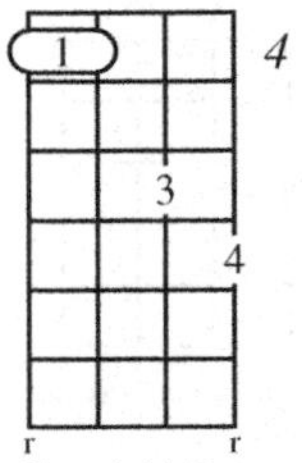

Closed 4th Pos

B

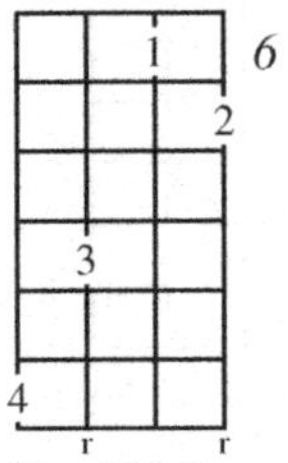

Closed 6th Pos

B

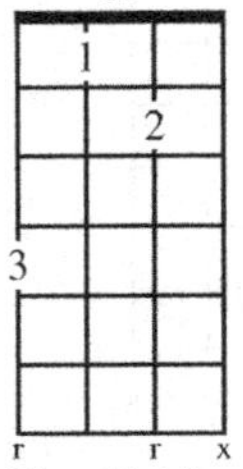

Closed 1st Pos

Dominant Seventh Chords

C7

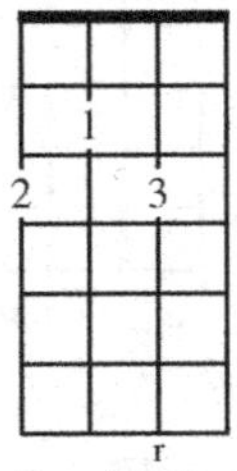

Open 2nd Pos

C7

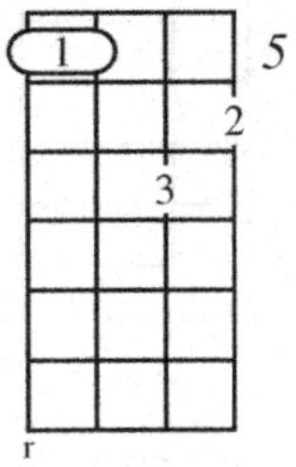

Closed 5th Pos

C7

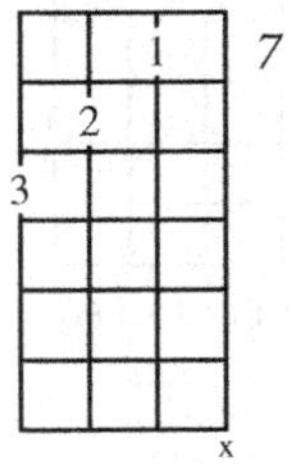

Closed 7th Pos

C7

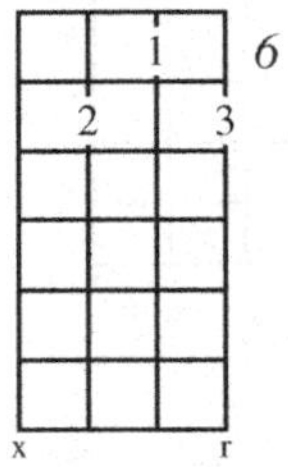

Closed 6th Pos

C7

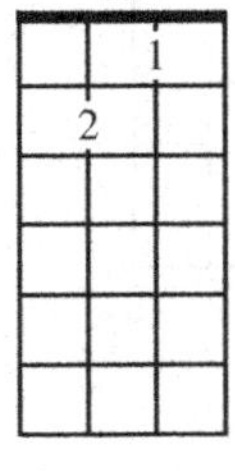

Open 1st Pos

C7

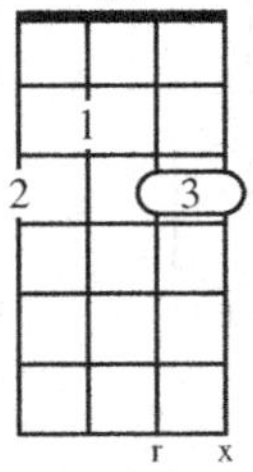

Closed 2nd Pos

C♯7/D♭7

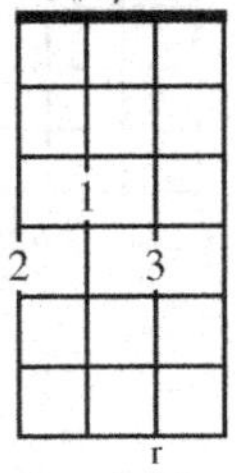

Open 3rd Pos

C♯7/D♭7

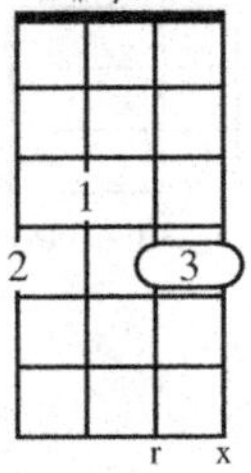

Closed 3rd Pos

C♯7/D♭7

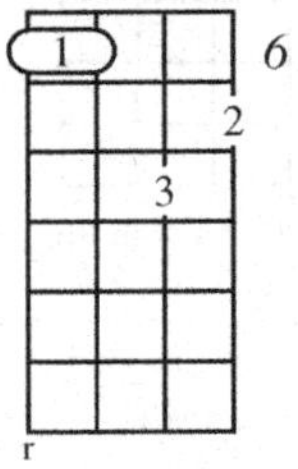

Closed 6th Pos

C♯7/D♭7

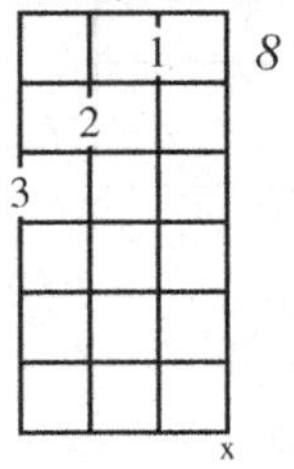

Closed 8th Pos

C♯7/D♭7

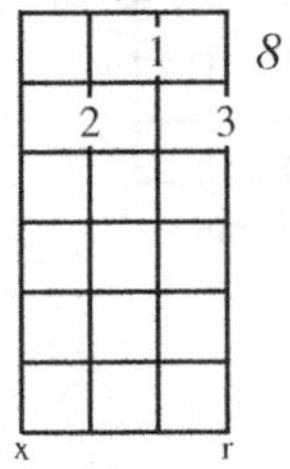

Closed 8th Pos

D7

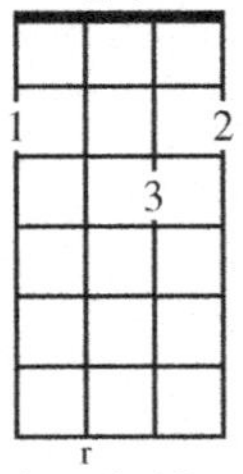

Open 2nd Pos

D7
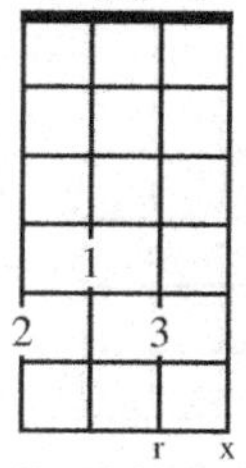
Closed 4th Pos

D7
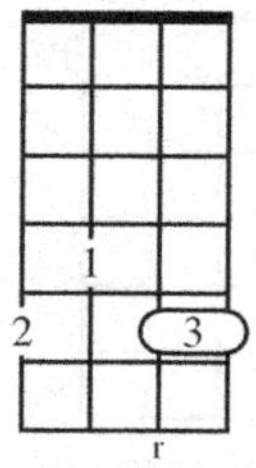
Closed 4th Pos

D7
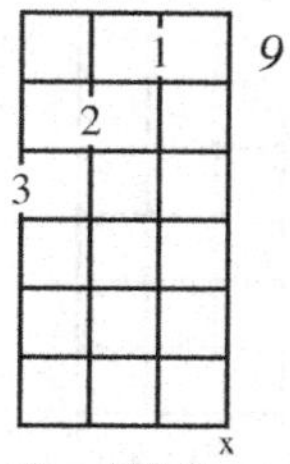
Closed 9th Pos

D7
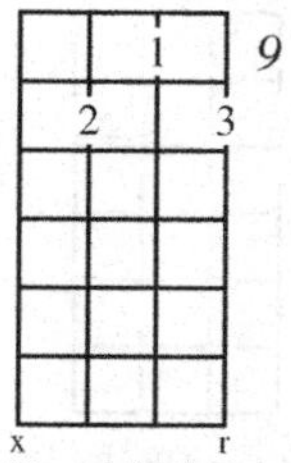
Closed 9th Pos

D7
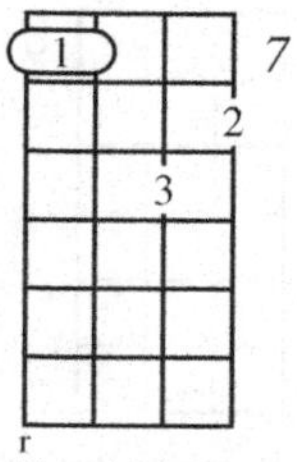
Closed 7th Pos

D♯7/E♭7
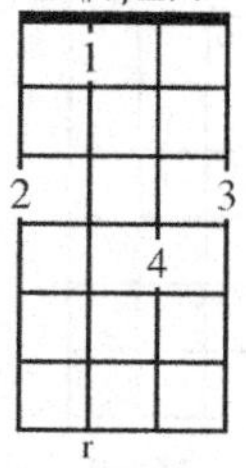
Closed 1st Pos

D♯7/E♭7
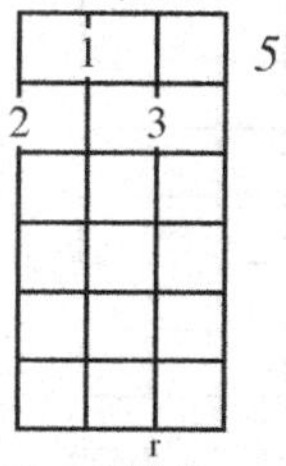
Closed 5th Pos

D♯7/E♭7
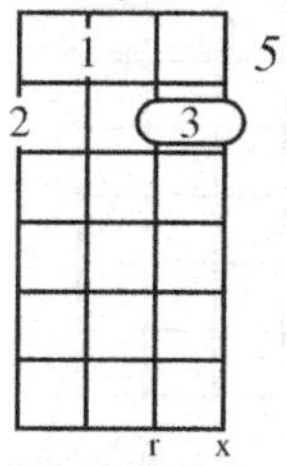
Closed 5th Pos

D♯7/E♭7
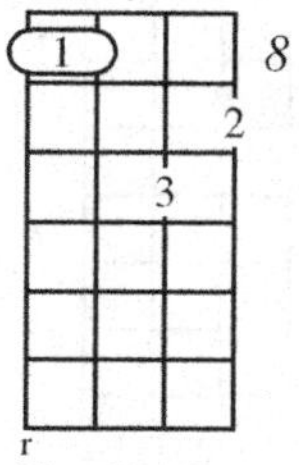
Closed 8th Pos

D♯7/E♭7
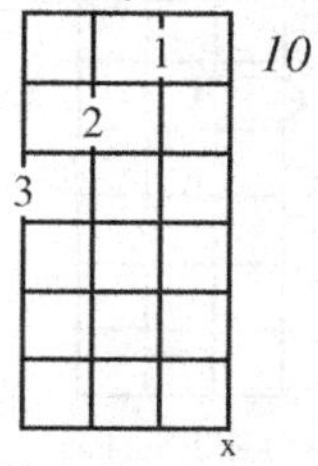
Closed 10th Pos

D♯7/E♭7
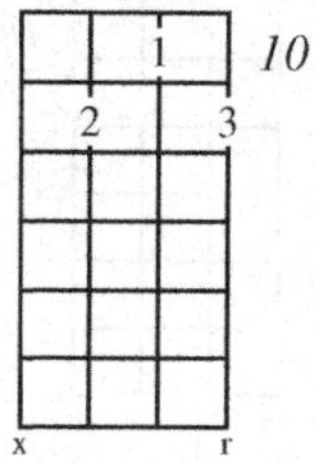
Closed 10th Pos

E7
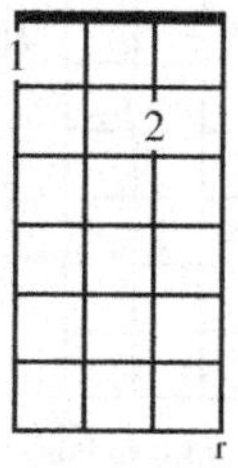
Open 1st Pos

E7
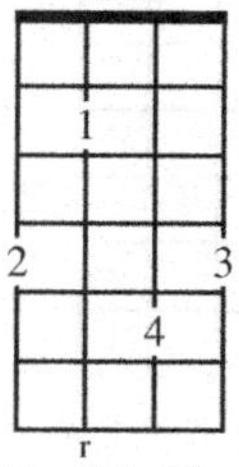
Closed 2nd Pos

E7
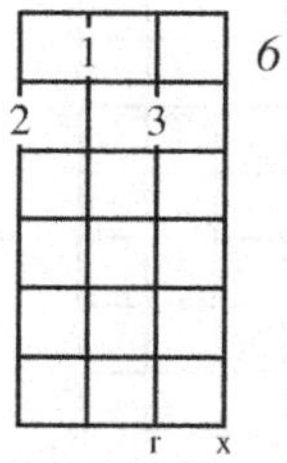
Closed 6th Pos

E7
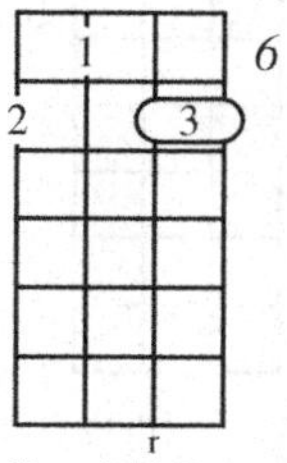
Closed 6th Pos

E7
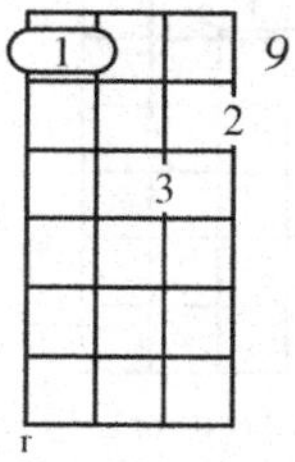
Closed 9th Pos

E7
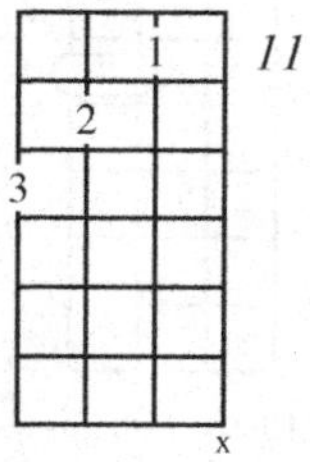
Closed 11th Pos

E7
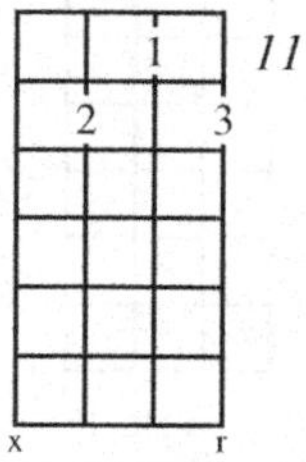
Closed 11th Pos

F7
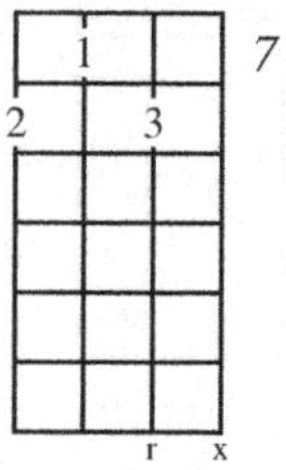
Closed 7th Pos

F7
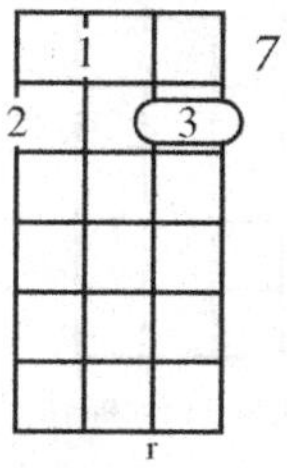
Closed 7th Pos

F7
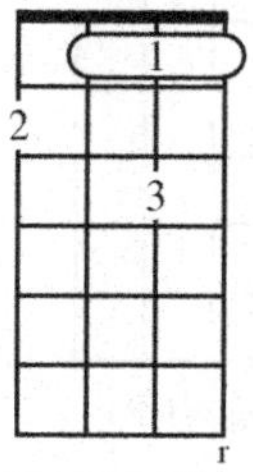
Closed 1st Pos

F7
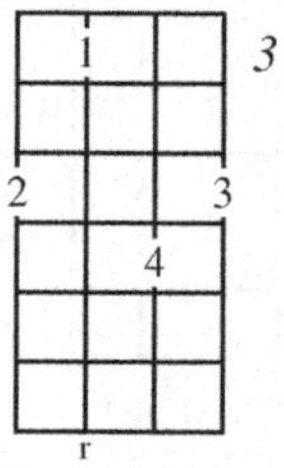
Closed 3rd Pos

F7
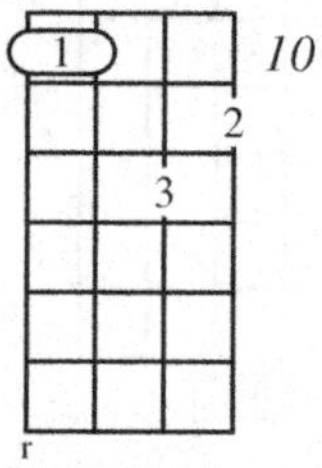
Closed 10th Pos

F♯7/G♭7
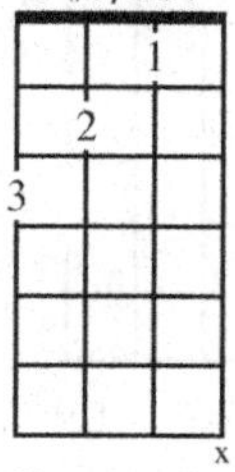
Closed 1st Pos

F♯7/G♭7
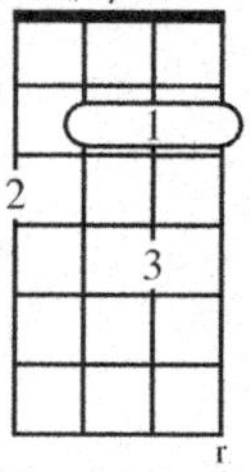
Closed 2nd Pos

F♯7/G♭7
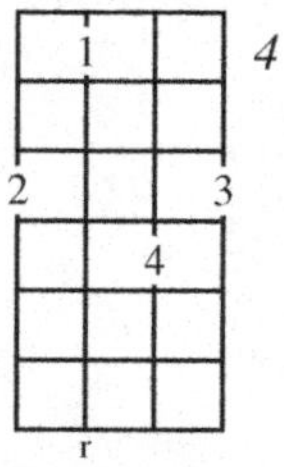
Closed 4th Pos

F♯7/G♭7
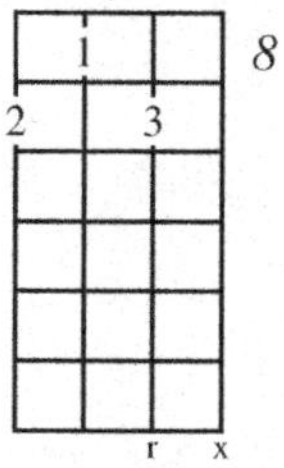
Closed 8th Pos

F♯7/G♭7
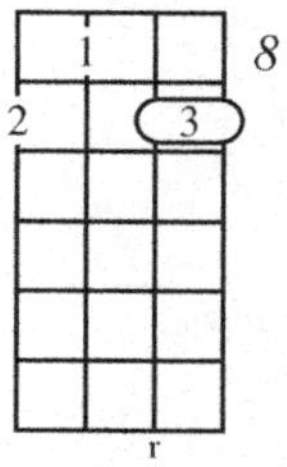
Closed 8th Pos

G7
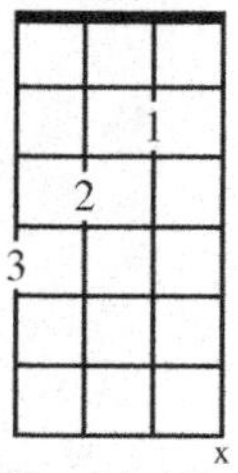
Closed 2nd Pos

G7
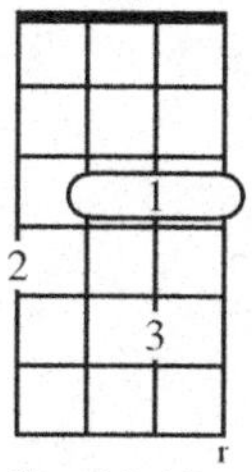
Closed 3rd Pos

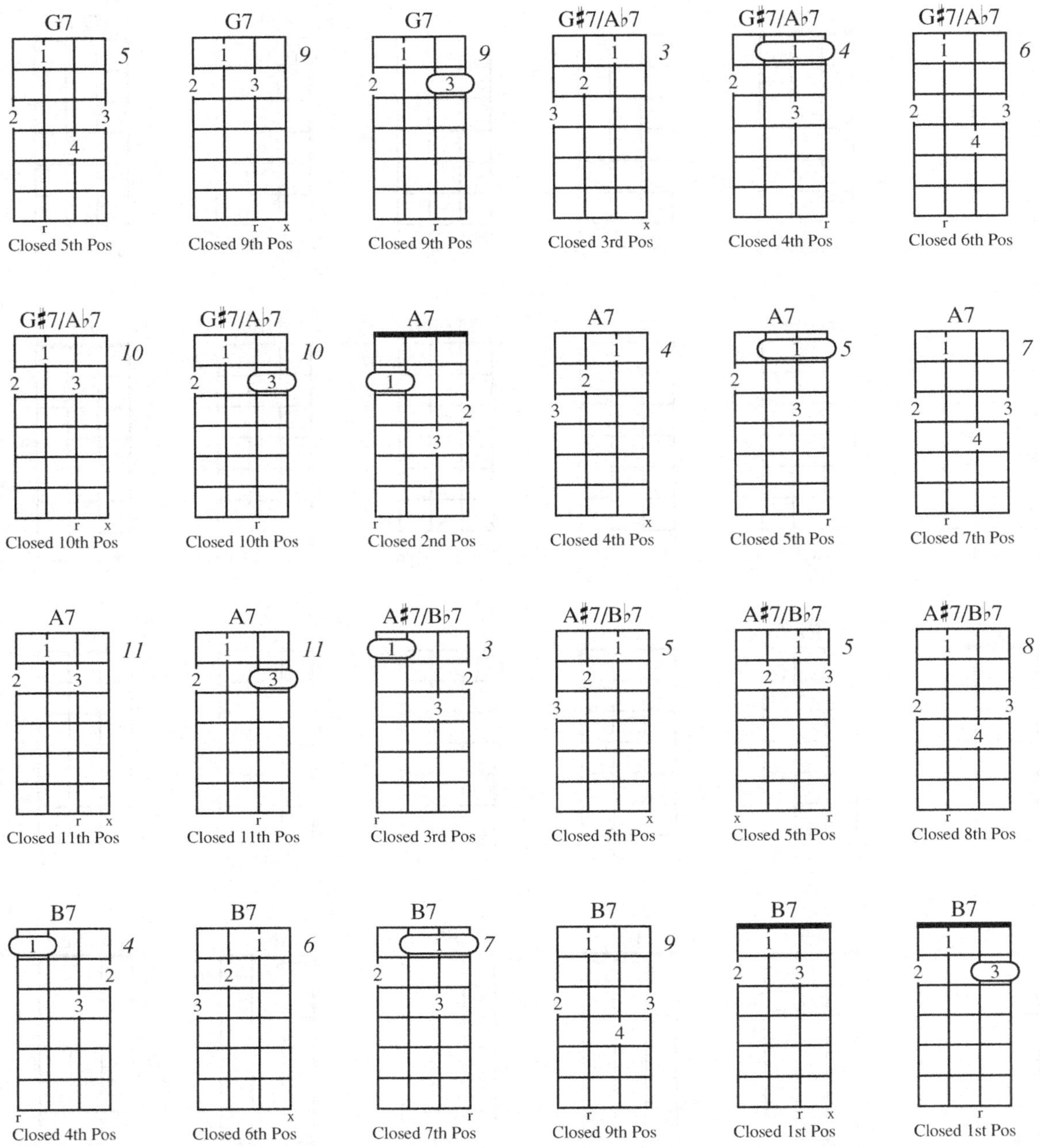
G7 5 Closed 5th Pos
G7 9 Closed 9th Pos
G7 9 Closed 9th Pos
G♯7/A♭7 3 Closed 3rd Pos
G♯7/A♭7 4 Closed 4th Pos
G♯7/A♭7 6 Closed 6th Pos
G♯7/A♭7 10 Closed 10th Pos
G♯7/A♭7 10 Closed 10th Pos
A7 Closed 2nd Pos
A7 4 Closed 4th Pos
A7 5 Closed 5th Pos
A7 7 Closed 7th Pos
A7 11 Closed 11th Pos
A7 11 Closed 11th Pos
A♯7/B♭7 3 Closed 3rd Pos
A♯7/B♭7 5 Closed 5th Pos
A♯7/B♭7 5 Closed 5th Pos
A♯7/B♭7 8 Closed 8th Pos
B7 4 Closed 4th Pos
B7 6 Closed 6th Pos
B7 7 Closed 7th Pos
B7 9 Closed 9th Pos
B7 Closed 1st Pos
B7 Closed 1st Pos

Minor Chords

Cm
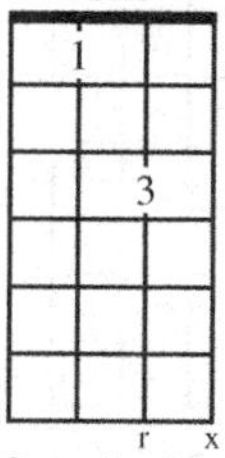
Open 1st Pos

Cm
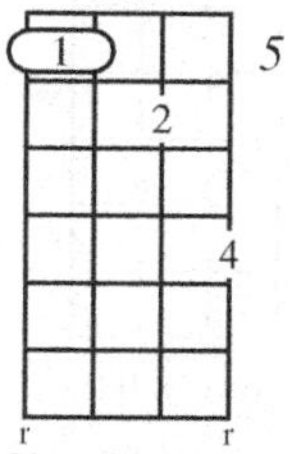
Closed 5th Pos

Cm
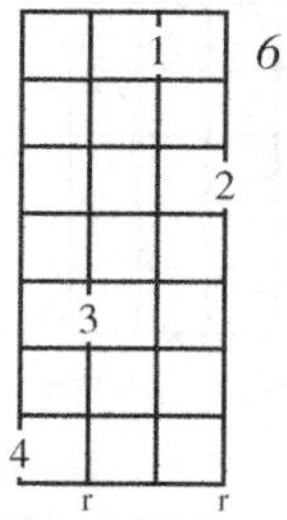
Closed 6th Pos

C♯m/D♭m
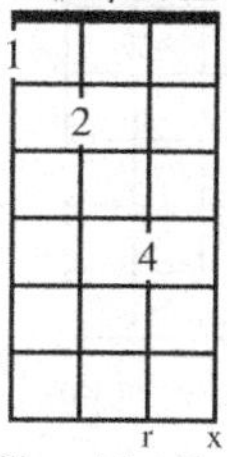
Closed 1st Pos

C♯m/D♭m
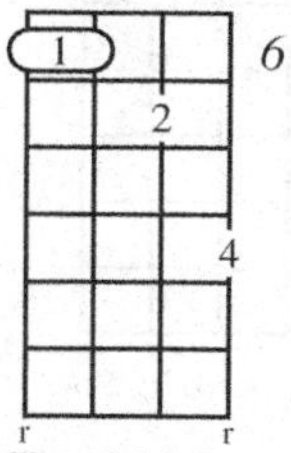
Closed 6th Pos

C♯m/D♭m
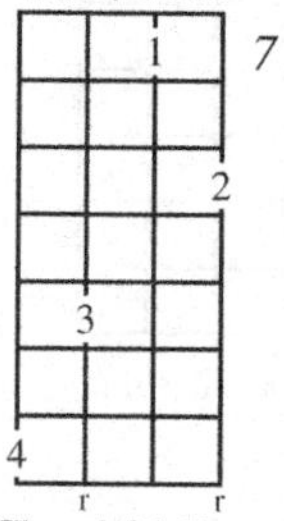
Closed 7th Pos

Dm
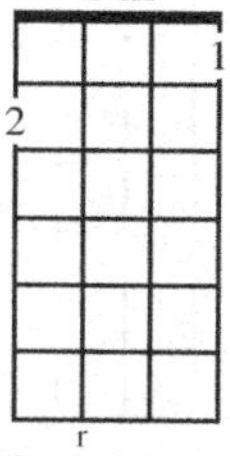
Open 1st Pos

Dm
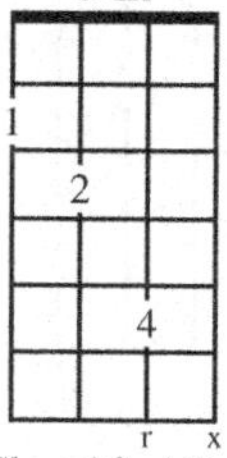
Closed 2nd Pos

Dm
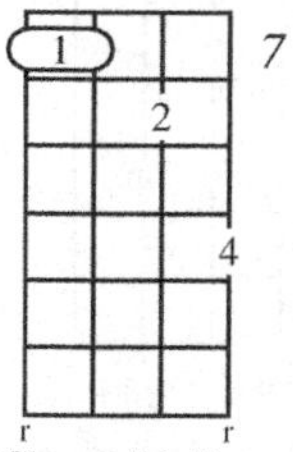
Closed 7th Pos

Dm
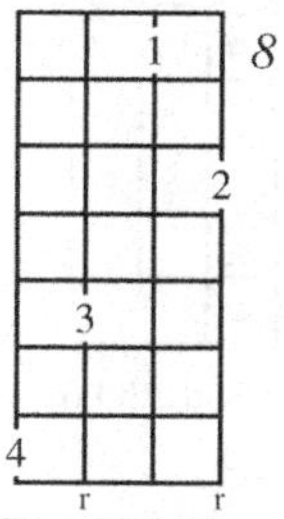
Closed 8th Pos

D♯m/E♭m
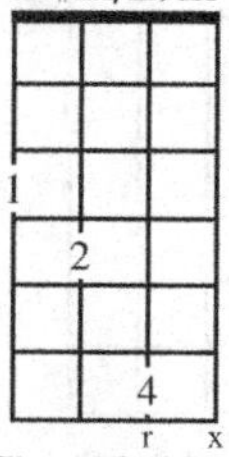
Closed 3rd Pos

D♯m/E♭m
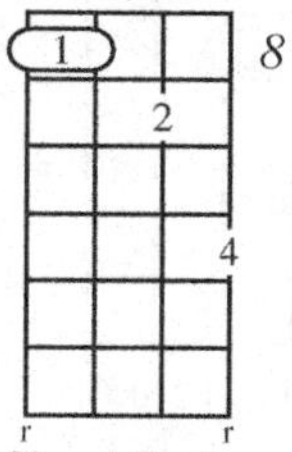
Closed 8th Pos

Em
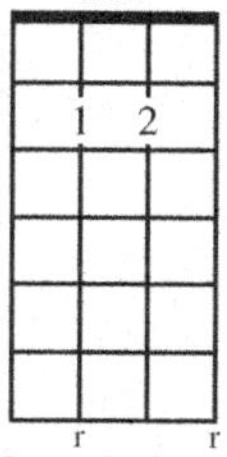
Open 2nd Pos

Em
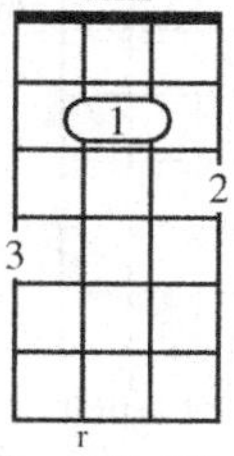
Closed 2nd Pos

Em
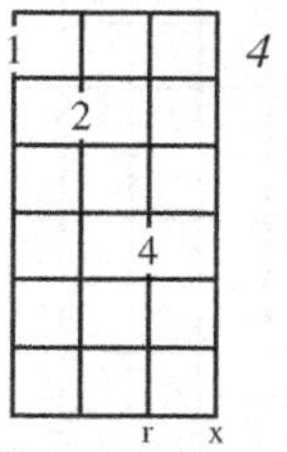
Closed 4th Pos

Em
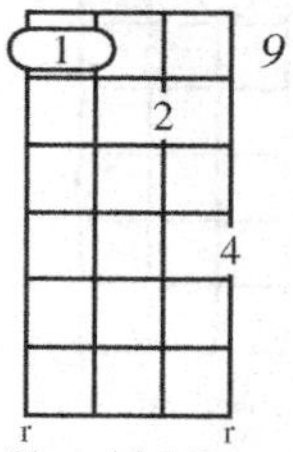
Closed 9th Pos

Fm
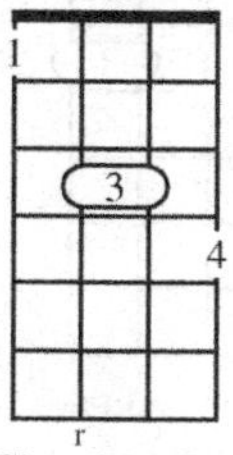
Closed 1st Pos

Fm
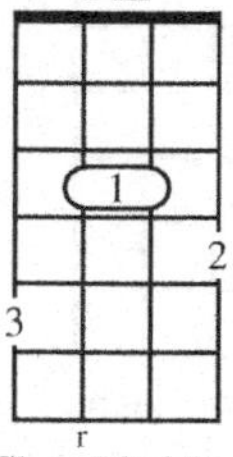
Closed 3rd Pos

Fm
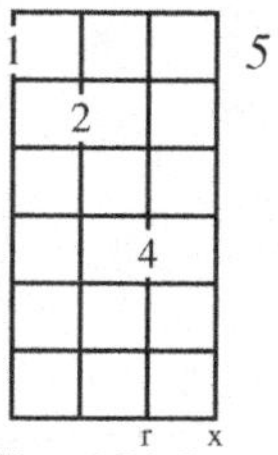
Closed 5th Pos

Fm
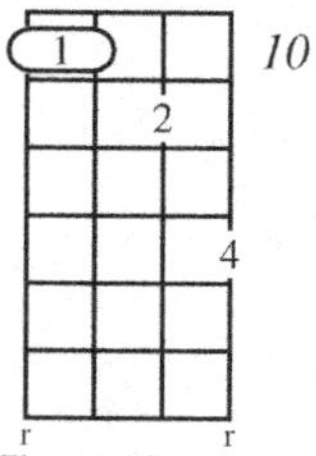
Closed 10th Pos

F♯m/G♭m
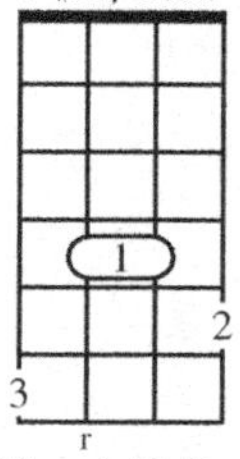
Closed 4th Pos

F♯m/G♭m
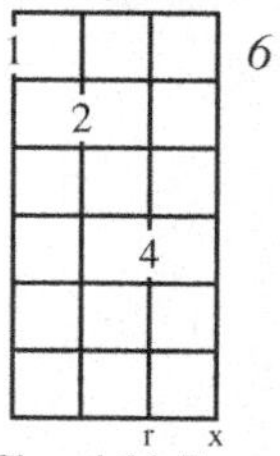
Closed 6th Pos

Gm
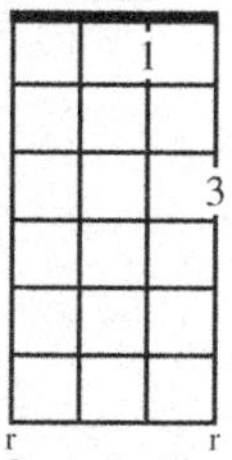
Open 1st Pos

Gm
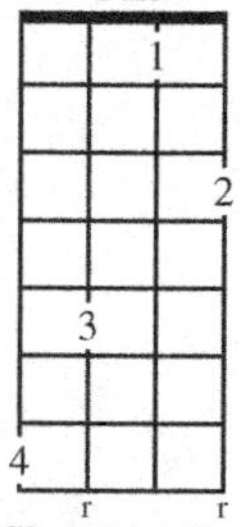
Closed 1st Pos

Gm

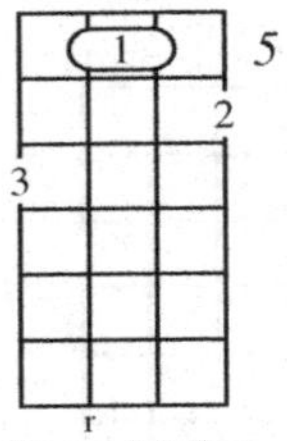

Closed 5th Pos

Gm

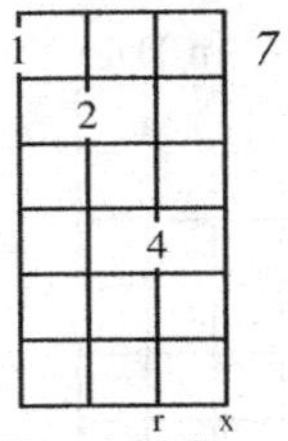

Closed 7th Pos

G♯m/A♭m

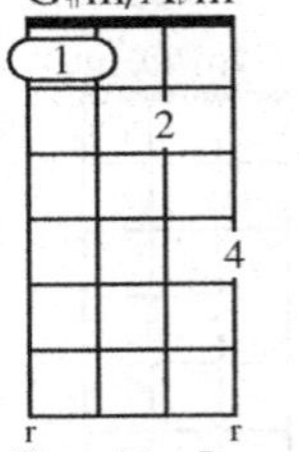

Closed 1st Pos

G♯m/A♭m

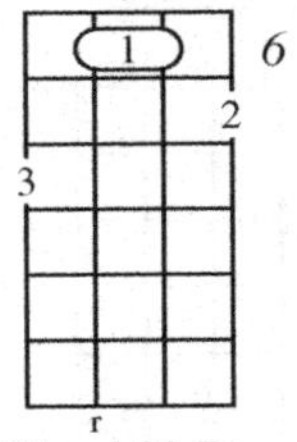

Closed 6th Pos

G♯m/A♭m

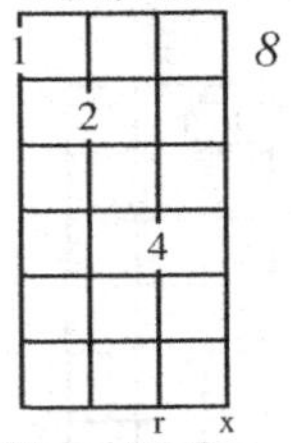

Closed 8th Pos

G♯m/A♭m

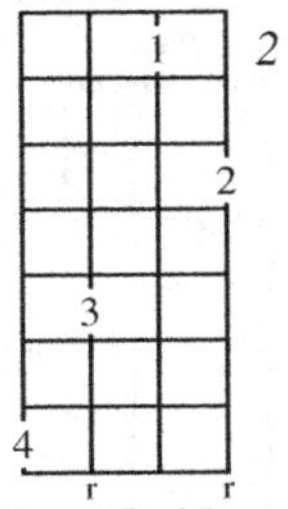

Closed 2nd Pos

Am

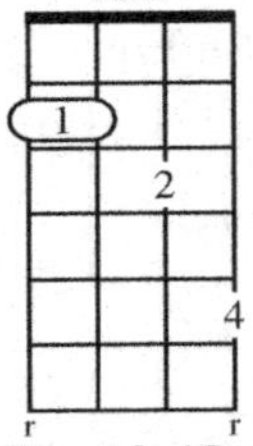

Closed 2nd Pos

Am

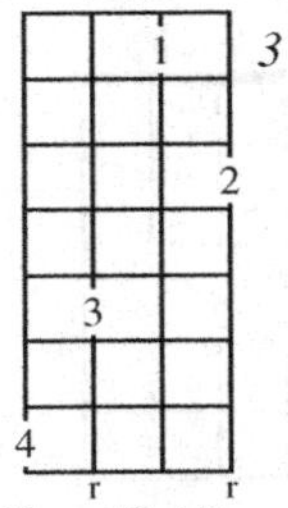

Closed 3rd Pos

Am

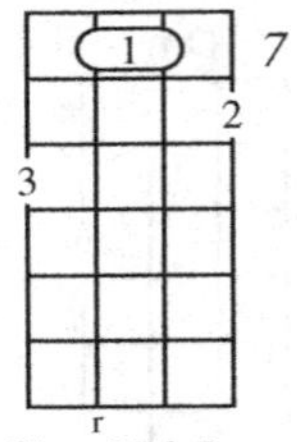

Closed 7th Pos

Am

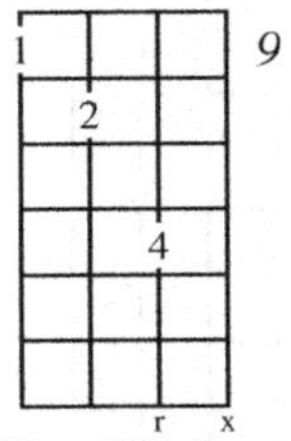

Closed 9th Pos

A♯m/B♭m

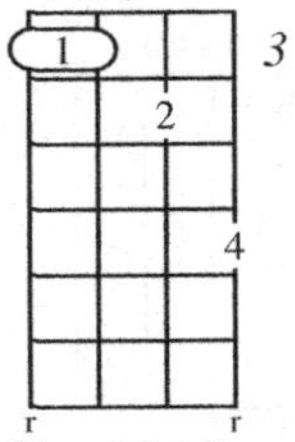

Closed 3rd Pos

A♯m/B♭m

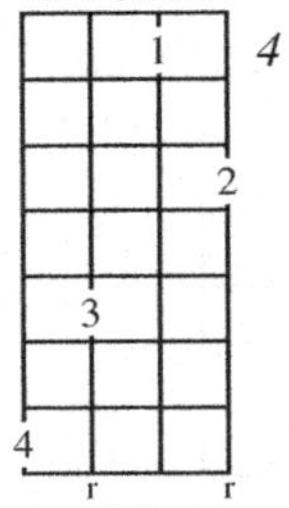

Closed 4th Pos

A♯m/B♭m

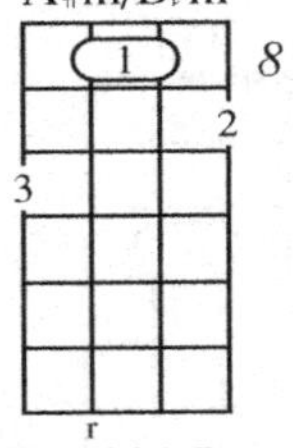

Closed 8th Pos

Bm

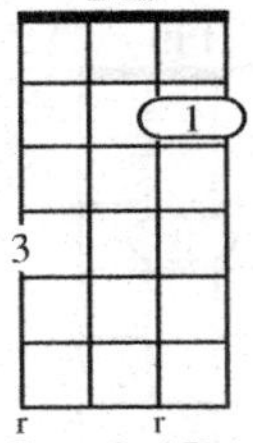

Open 2nd Pos

Bm

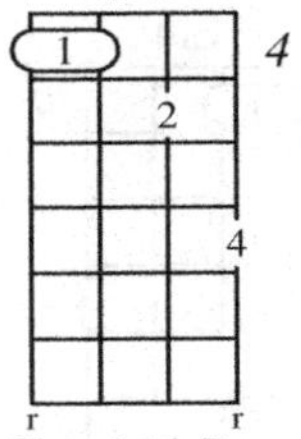

Closed 4th Pos

Bm

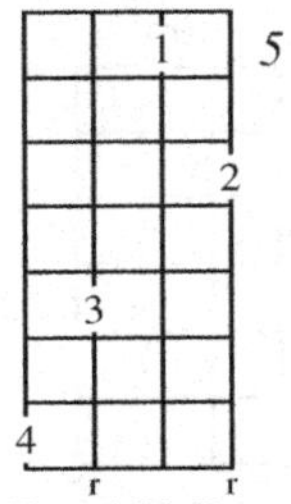

Closed 5th Pos

Bm

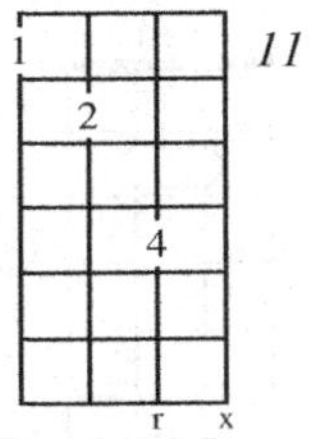

Closed 11th Pos

Index

BILL'S MUSIC SHELF

UNIQUELY INTERESTING MUSIC!

Made in the USA
Las Vegas, NV
09 October 2025

32084721R00039